The United States

New Jersey

Anne Welsbacher
ABDO & Daughters

visit us at
www.abdopub.com

Published by Abdo & Daughters, 4940 Viking Drive, Suite 622, Edina, Minnesota 55435.
Copyright © 1998 by Abdo Consulting Group, Inc., Pentagon Tower, P.O. Box 36036,
Minneapolis, Minnesota 55435 USA. International copyrights reserved in all countries.
No part of this book may be reproduced in any form without written permission from the
publisher.

Printed in the United States.

Cover and Interior Photo credits: Peter Arnold, Inc., SuperStock, Archive, Corbis-
Bettmann

Edited by Lori Kinstad Pupeza
Contributing editor Brooke Henderson
Special thanks to our Checkerboard Kids—Peter Rengstorf, Peter Dumdei, Shane
Wagner, Priscilla Cáceres

Population statistics taken from the 2000 census, U.S. Census Bureau.

Library of Congress Cataloging-in-Publication Data

Welsbacher, Anne, 1955-
      New Jersey / Anne Welsbacher.
      p. cm. -- (United States)
      Includes index.
      Summary: Examines the history, geography, cities, recreations, and industries of
      the Garden State.
      ISBN 1-56239-892-X
      1. New Jersey--Juvenile literature. [1. New Jersey.] I. Title. II. Series:
      United States (Series)
      F134.3.W45 1998
      974.9--dc21   97-34112
                                                                             CIP
                                                                             AC

Contents

Welcome to New Jersey

The small state of New Jersey is surrounded by the ocean, a big river, and a big bay. Big states like New York and Pennsylvania are on either side. But little New Jersey is a big part of the United States.

Many battles were fought against England in New Jersey. New Jersey has many sports teams. New Jersey makes more **chemicals** than any other state.

And New Jersey has a lot of people! Most people live in the cities. But New Jersey has many pretty farms and flowers, too. For this reason, New Jersey is called the Garden State.

Opposite page: Delaware water gap national recreation area, New Jersey.

Fast Facts

NEW JERSEY

Capital
Trenton (85,403 people)
Area
7,468 square miles
(19,342 sq km)
Population
8,414,350 people
Rank: 9th
Statehood
December 18, 1787
(3rd state admitted)
Principal river
Delaware River
Highest point
High Point;
1,803 feet (550 m)
Largest city
Newark (273,546 people)
Motto
Liberty and prosperity
Famous People
Count Basie, James Fenimore
Cooper, Thomas Edison, Albert
Einstein, Molly Pitcher, Paul
Robeson, Frank Sinatra, Bruce
Springsteen, Walt Whitman

New Jersey is one of the original 13 colonies

13

*P*urple Violet

*S*tate Flag

*E*astern Gold Finch

*R*ed Oak

About New Jersey

The Garden State

Detail area

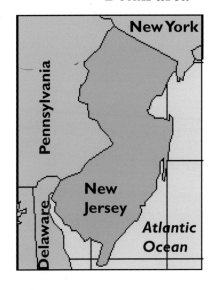

New Jersey's
abbreviation

Borders: west (Pennsylvania, Delaware), north (New York),
east (New York, Atlantic Ocean), south (Atlantic Ocean)

Nature's Treasures

New Jersey's greatest treasure is where it is! New Jersey is between the ocean and the rest of the country, and between big cities like New York and Philadelphia. So many things move to New Jersey on ships, and then across New Jersey on its many trains and roads.

New Jersey has many forests. Some of the trees are cut down. The wood is used as lumber.

New Jersey's land has granite, sand, and gravel. Other treasures in the land are clay, **peat**, and zinc. Sand and gravel are made into cement, which is used to build things.

The weather in New Jersey is warm or hot in the summer and cold in the winter. Along the coast, the ocean water breezes cool the air in the summer and warm the air in the winter.

Gateway National Park, New Jersey.

Beginnings

About 10,000 years ago, Native Americans lived in the area now called New Jersey. They were called the Lenni-Lenape people. They hunted and grew corn and other food. In the 1600s, settlers from Europe started to come to the new land. They pushed the Native Americans out of the area.

In 1776, New Jersey and other **colonies** signed a paper called the Declaration of Independence. Then they fought and won the Revolutionary War against England. They became the United States of America. In 1787, New Jersey became the third state of the new United States of America.

Many of the Revolution's battles were fought in New Jersey. One reason is because the states on either side of New Jersey, which were New York and Pennsylvania, were big colonies that both sides wanted. So New Jersey got in the middle of the fighting!

In the 1800s, New Jersey began building many roads and railroads. **Turnpikes** also were built.

Factories grew. Saddles, tools, paper, and many other things were made in the factories. New Jersey farms grew fruits and vegetables. All these things were shipped to other states on the many roads and trains in New Jersey.

As factories grew, so did the cities. They were full of people! In the 1900s, new companies grew. Today in Atlantic City, many people come to visit its famous Boardwalk and swim in the ocean.

The Battle of Princeton, during the American Revolution.

1600s to 1775

Early Times

 1600s: The Lenni-Lenape people live in the New Jersey area. Dutch, Swedish, and English settlers arrive.

 1666: Newark is **founded**. It is one of the oldest big cities in the United States.

 1746: Princeton University is opened. It is one of the oldest **colleges** in the United States.

 1775: War begins between American **colonies** and England. Many battles are fought in New Jersey.

New Jersey

1600s to 1775

1781 to Early 1800s

A New Country

 1781: The war with England ends. The United States of America is born. A peace treaty is signed in 1783.

 1787: New Jersey becomes the third state.

 Early 1800s: Many repairs are made in New Jersey after the war. New bridges, **canals**, roads, and railroads are built.

New Jersey

1781 to Early 1800s

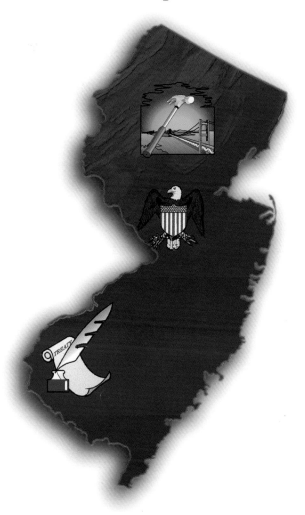

1880s to 1978

People and Parks

1880s: Many **immigrants** come to New Jersey from Italy, Poland, Russia, and other countries.

1900s: Big factories are built. More and more people live in cities because they can get jobs at the factories.

1952: The New Jersey **Turnpike** opens. It is one of the busiest highways in the United States.

1978: Casino Gambling becomes legal. Also, the New Jersey Pinelands, one of many parks in New Jersey, is made a protected national park. It is one of the largest parks in the United States.

New Jersey

1880s to 1978

Trenton

New Jersey's People

There are 8.4 million people in New Jersey. Only eight states in the country have more people. Yet only four states are smaller than New Jersey! Most New Jerseyans live in cities.

Singers Whitney Houston and Paul Simon are from Newark. Bruce Springsteen was born in Freehold. Dionne Warwick was born in East Orange, New Jersey.

Frank Sinatra was born in Hoboken. And jazz greats Count Basie and Sarah Vaughan were both from the Garden State.

John Travolta is from Englewood, New Jersey. Jack Nicholson is from Neptune. Meryl Streep is from Basking Ridge. And John Amos is from Newark. All four are actors.

Writers Judy Blume, James Fenimore Cooper, and Stephen Crane were born in New Jersey. So were poets Allen Ginsburg and William Carlos Williams.

Virginia Apgar was from Westfield. She was a doctor who made up a new way to check the health of newborn babies. Astronaut Edwin Aldrin, the comedy team Abbott and Costello, actor Paul Robeson, and cartoonist Charles Addams all were born in New Jersey.

Judy Blume

Edwin "Buzz" Aldrin

Whitney Houston

New Jersey's Cities

Newark is the largest city in New Jersey. It is in the northeast part of the state. It is near the ocean, and ships come and go. There also is an airport in Newark that sends planes all over the world.

Nearby Jersey City is the next largest. Liberty State Park is in Jersey City, near the Statue of Liberty.

Paterson is the third largest city in New Jersey. Samuel Colt began making guns, called Colt revolvers, in Paterson. Many trains were made in Paterson, too.

Elizabeth is the fourth largest city. The **inventor** Thomas Edison lived in Newark. Farther south is Camden. North of Camden is Trenton. It is the capital of New Jersey.

Atlantic City, next to the ocean, has a long wooden sidewalk called the Boardwalk. There are many fun things to do along the Boardwalk. Many people from all over the country visit Atlantic City every year.

Atlantic City, New Jersey.

New Jersey's Land

New Jersey is shaped like a seahorse. This is a good shape for New Jersey, because it has water all around it! New Jersey's land is divided into four different regions. The Kittatinny Mountain region covers the northwestern part of the state. This mostly mountain area is part of the Appalachian chain. In this region there are also rivers and forests. The highest point in the state is called High Point, it's in this region.

The Highlands region is covered with wooded hills and dotted with lakes. The region has the largest natural body of water, Lake Hopatcong.

The Piedmont Plateau is in the middle of the state. It has gentle hills and many waterfalls. This region is filled with many rivers.

In the middle and southern parts of New Jersey is the Coastal Plain. It is the largest region. There are pine forests and swamp land. This region also is excellent for growing vegetables and fruit.

Throughout the state, New Jersey's forests are filled with beech, birch, maple, oak, and pine trees. Purple violet, honeysuckle, goldenrod, buttercups, Queen Anne's lace, and Virginia cowslips are a few of the many flowers that grow in the Garden State.

Island Beach State Park, New Jersey.

New Jersey at Play

There's lots to do on the New Jersey coast. People swim, surf, build sand castles, and hunt for seashells. Many people visit the Boardwalk in Atlantic City.

New Jerseyans love sports! The New York Giants and the New York Jets football teams play in New Jersey. The New Jersey Nets play basketball and the New Jersey Devils are the state hockey team.

There are more than 50 parks and forests in New Jersey. At Liberty State Park, visitors can see New York City and the Atlantic ocean. One trail in the big Pinelands park is 48 miles (77 km) long!

In Morristown, visitors can see forts and camps from the Revolutionary War. Thomas Edison lived and **invented** new things in West Orange.

Each September, the Miss America contest is held in Atlantic City. In March, the New Jersey Flower and Garden Show is in Morristown. In May, there are dog shows in Trenton. In June, Wildwood hosts a marbles contest!

Barnegat Lighthouse State Park, New Jersey.

New Jersey at Work

Many New Jerseyans work in **manufacturing**. They make **chemicals**, soaps, and medicine.

Some New Jerseyans like to fish. They catch clams, lobsters, and sea bass. New Jerseyans also work in hotels, motels, and places to eat.

The Garden State has many gardeners! They work in greenhouses, and keep plants alive in special heated glass rooms. They also grow roses and other flowers, as well as fruits like peaches and blueberries.

Opposite page: Boats at a pier in
Highlands, New Jersey.

Fun Facts

• The first dinosaur skeleton found in North America, in 1858, was in New Jersey. It was the skeleton of a hadrosaur.

• Women had the right to vote in New Jersey beginning in 1776, when the right was written down in a law. But in 1807, New Jersey leaders took away the right. Women did not re-win their right to vote for more than 100 years.

• The first drive-in movie theater opened in Camden, New Jersey, in 1933.

• The game Monopoly was **invented** in 1933 by Charles Darrow. He named the streets in the game for the streets in the real Atlantic City, where there is a sign in honor of him.

• New Jersey's Sandy Hook Lighthouse was first lit in 1764, and has been used ever since, longer than any other lighthouse in the United States.

•The electric light bulb was **invented** by Thomas Edison in Menlo Park, New Jersey, in 1879. Edison also invented the talking doll and wax paper!

•One of the first long-distance telephone calls was made from New Jersey to New York in 1877.

•Atlantic City is famous for its saltwater taffy. Saltwater taffy got its name after a big ocean wave came up and covered a taffy stand with salty sea water!

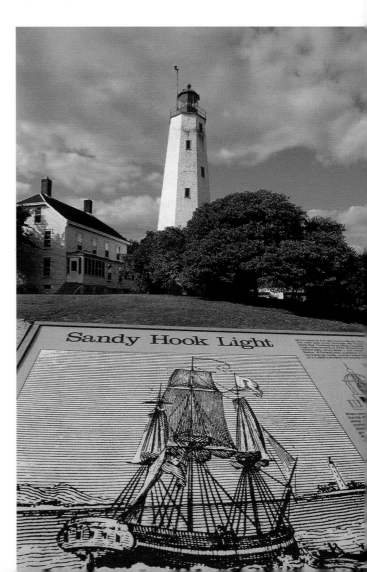

Sandy Hook Lighthouse, New Jersey.

Glossary

Border: the edge of something.

Canal: a small river made by people, lined with cement; people can "drive" boats through a canal just like they drive cars on a street.

Chemical: something used in chemistry; oxygen is a chemical that is in the air. This chemical allows all living things to live and breathe.

Claim: to take.

College: a school you can go to after high school; a university is a kind of college.

Colony: a place owned by another country.

Founded: to bring into being; to start or set up a new city.

Immigrant: a person who moves to a country from another country.

Invent: to make something for the first time.

Invention: something that is invented.

Manufacture: to make things.

Mineral: something like coal or diamonds that is in the earth.

Peat: rotted plants found in swamps. Peat is used as a fertilizer.

Smallpox: a kind of sickness that came to the United States with people from England and other places; many Native Americans died from this disease.

Turnpike: a highway that drivers pay to ride on.

Internet Sites

New Jersey Online
http://www.nj.com/
This site is very colorful and interactive. It includes Sports Talk, News Report, Jersey Talk, weather, politics, and eduction. This is one of the best websites for links to cool spots. Check it out.

New Jersey: The Center of the Universe
http://www.cnj.digex.net/~lars/center.html
As it turns out, the center of the universe is located somewhere between Southern New York and Northern Delaware. That's right. The center of the universe is New Jersey. Unbelievable as it seems, The Garden State is the center of all we know. Scientists have requested that a blue ribbon commitee be put together to catalog everything we know. One scientist had a better idea. What better place to do it then the World Wide Web? But who could handle it? Who would want to?! They knew who.

These sites are subject to change. Go to your favorite search engine and type in New Jersey for more sites.

PASS IT ON
Tell Others Something Special About Your State

To educate readers around the country, pass on interesting tips, places to see, history, and little unknown facts about the state you live in. We want to hear from you!
To get posted on ABDO & Daughters website, e-mail us at "mystate@abdopub.com"

Index